IT'S TIME TO LEARN ABOUT CLOWN FISH

It's Time to Learn about Clown Fish

Walter the Educator

Silent King Books
A WhichHead Entertainment Imprint

Copyright © 2025 by Walter the Educator

All rights reserved. No part of this book may be reproduced in any manner whatsoever without written per- mission except in the case of brief quotations embodied in critical articles and reviews.

First Printing, 2024

Disclaimer

This book is a literary work; the story is not about specific persons, locations, situations, and/or circumstances unless mentioned in a historical context. Any resemblance to real persons, locations, situations, and/or circumstances is coincidental. This book is for entertainment and informational purposes only. The author and publisher offer this information without warranties expressed or implied. No matter the grounds, neither the author nor the publisher will be accountable for any losses, injuries, or other damages caused by the reader's use of this book. The use of this book acknowledges an understanding and acceptance of this disclaimer.

It's Time to Learn about Clown Fish is a collectible early learning book by Walter the Educator suitable for all ages belonging to Walter the Educator's Time to Eat Book Series. Collect more books at WaltertheEducator.com

USE THE EXTRA SPACE TO TAKE NOTES AND DOCUMENT YOUR MEMORIES

CLOWN FISH

Down in the sea where the bright corals grow,

It's Time to Learn about

Clown Fish

Lives a small fish with a bright orange glow.

With stripes of white like a zebra's coat,

It swims through the water as if it can float!

This fish is a clown, but not from a show,

It's called a clownfish — now you know!

It wiggles and giggles through sea anemones,

Safe from the stingers that sway in the breeze.

The anemone's arms are quite sticky and smart,

But not to the clownfish — they know their part!

They make a good team, both fish and flower,

Protecting each other hour by hour.

Clownfish are tiny, not very tall,

Some are so little, they're smaller than a ball!

They stay close to home and don't roam too wide,

Their wavy anemone is where they hide.

Did you know clownfish can change if they wish?

If the queen fish is gone, a boy turns to a miss!

In clownfish towns, it's a clever old trick,

To keep their small families healthy and quick.

They chatter and chatter with clicks and pops,

It's Time to Learn about

Clown Fish

Making small noises that never quite stop.

It's how they talk to their friends each day,

In their splashy, bubbly, underwater way.

Clownfish eat shrimp and some tasty bits,

Tiny little creatures that the ocean admits.

They munch and they crunch and they nibble all day,

Swimming and smiling in a bright coral bay.

They have little fins that flap, flap, flap,

Like a tiny sailor adjusting their cap.

They dart left and right, they dance and they dive,

Always excited and feeling alive!

Some clownfish are orange, some yellow or pink,

Each with their own bright, beautiful wink.

Nature paints them in colors so fine,

Each clownfish shining like a sparkly sign.

So next time you see a clownfish wave,

Think of the ocean, bright and brave!

A tiny hero with stripes of delight,

It's Time to Learn about

Clown Fish

Playing and laughing from morning to night.

ABOUT THE CREATOR

Walter the Educator is one of the pseudonyms for Walter Anderson. Formally educated in Chemistry, Business, and Education, he is an educator, an author, a diverse entrepreneur, and he is the son of a disabled war veteran. "Walter the Educator" shares his time between educating and creating. He holds interests and owns several creative projects that entertain, enlighten, enhance, and educate, hoping to inspire and motivate you. Follow, find new works, and stay up to date with Walter the Educator™

at WaltertheEducator.com

www.ingramcontent.com/pod-product-compliance
Lightning Source LLC
LaVergne TN
LVHW010412070526
838199LV00064B/5266